Brimax Publishing
415 Jackson St, San Francisco
CA 94111 USA

Illustrated by Jenny Tulip
Copyright © Brimax Publishing, 2004
Printed in China  (June 2015) 10 9 8

# My First
# 500 Spanish Words

# Mis Primeras
# 500 palabras en español

# Introduction

Learning a new language helps you to communicate with people from other countries, so you can make friends, buy things at shops, ask for directions, read foreign books, and watch foreign films.

Enjoy the experience of learning Spanish together with your family and friends!

There are many countries in which people speak Spanish. The words found in this book are in Latin American Spanish, mainly in Mexican Spanish.

Topics range from numbers, days, months and seasons, shapes and colors, through to objects found in the garden, at the beach, at the shops, and even at the toy store!

# Introducción

Aprender otro idioma te ayudará a comunicarte con personas de otros países, y así podras hacer nuevos amigos, comprar cosas en los negocios, pedir indicaciones, leer libros y mirar películas en otros idiomas.

Disfruta de la experiencia de aprender español junto a tu familia y tus amigos!

Hay muchos países en los que se habla español. Sin embargo, las palabras que aparecen en este libro están en español latinoamericano y sobre todo mejicano.

Los temas en este libro varían desde números, días de la semana y meses y estaciones del año hasta objetos que se encuentran en el jardín, en la playa, en los negocios y hasta en la juguetería!

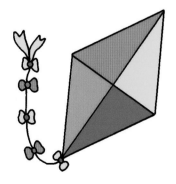

# Counting to twenty - Contando hasta viente

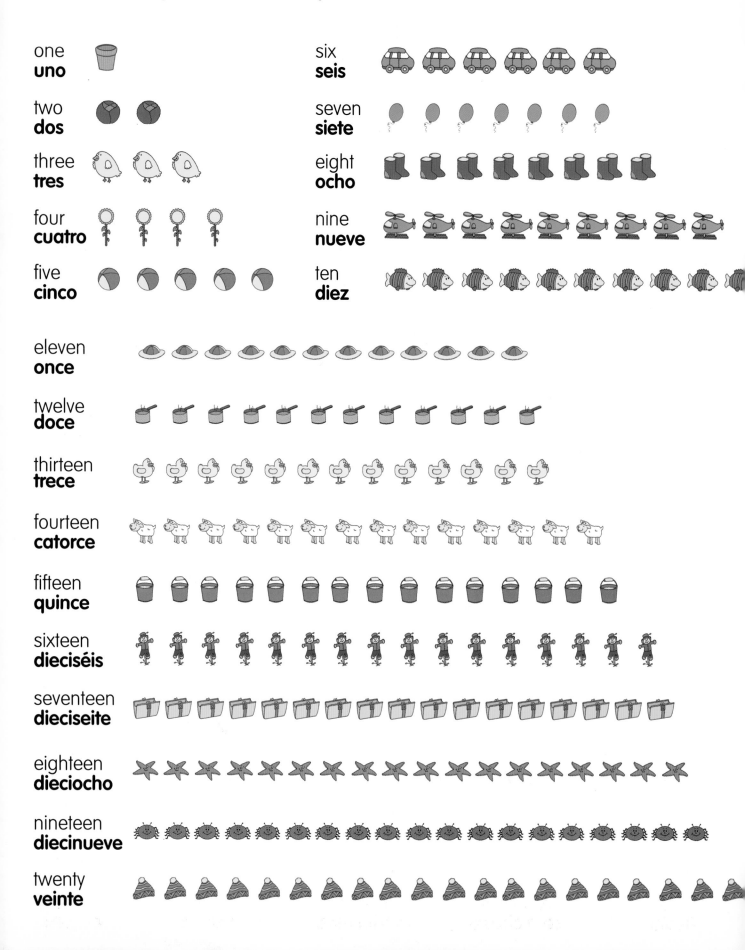

one
**uno**

six
**seis**

two
**dos**

seven
**siete**

three
**tres**

eight
**ocho**

four
**cuatro**

nine
**nueve**

five
**cinco**

ten
**diez**

eleven
**once**

twelve
**doce**

thirteen
**trece**

fourteen
**catorce**

fifteen
**quince**

sixteen
**dieciséis**

seventeen
**dieciseite**

eighteen
**dieciocho**

nineteen
**diecinueve**

twenty
**veinte**

# Shapes and Colors - Formas y Colores

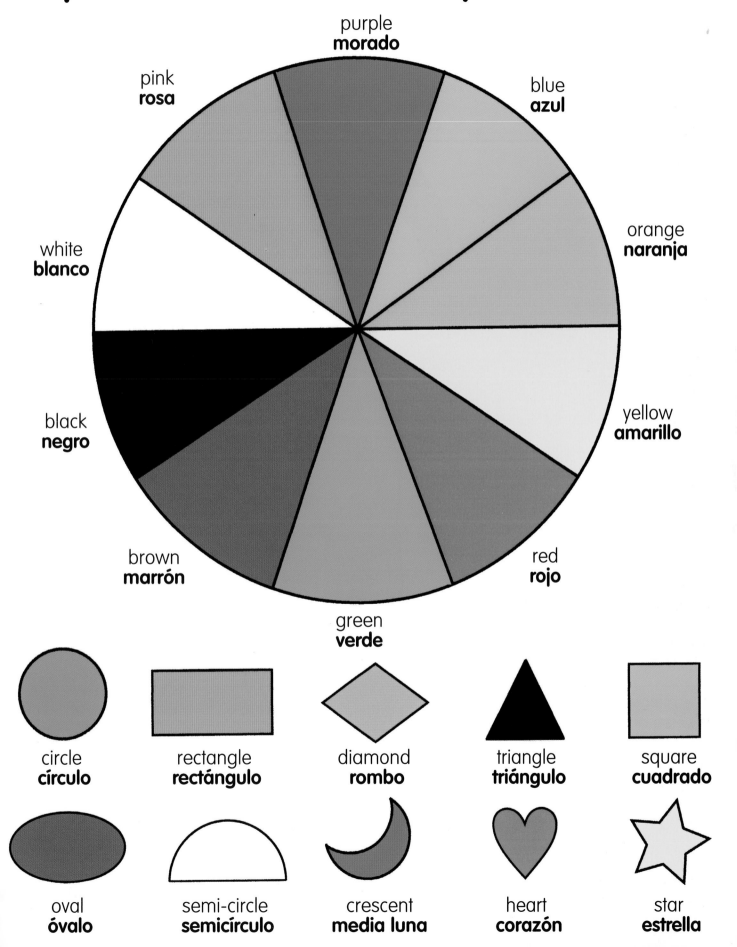

purple
**morado**

pink
**rosa**

blue
**azul**

white
**blanco**

orange
**naranja**

yellow
**amarillo**

black
**negro**

red
**rojo**

brown
**marrón**

green
**verde**

circle
**círculo**

rectangle
**rectángulo**

diamond
**rombo**

triangle
**triángulo**

square
**cuadrado**

oval
**óvalo**

semi-circle
**semicírculo**

crescent
**media luna**

heart
**corazón**

star
**estrella**

# Our Bodies - Nuestros Cuerpos

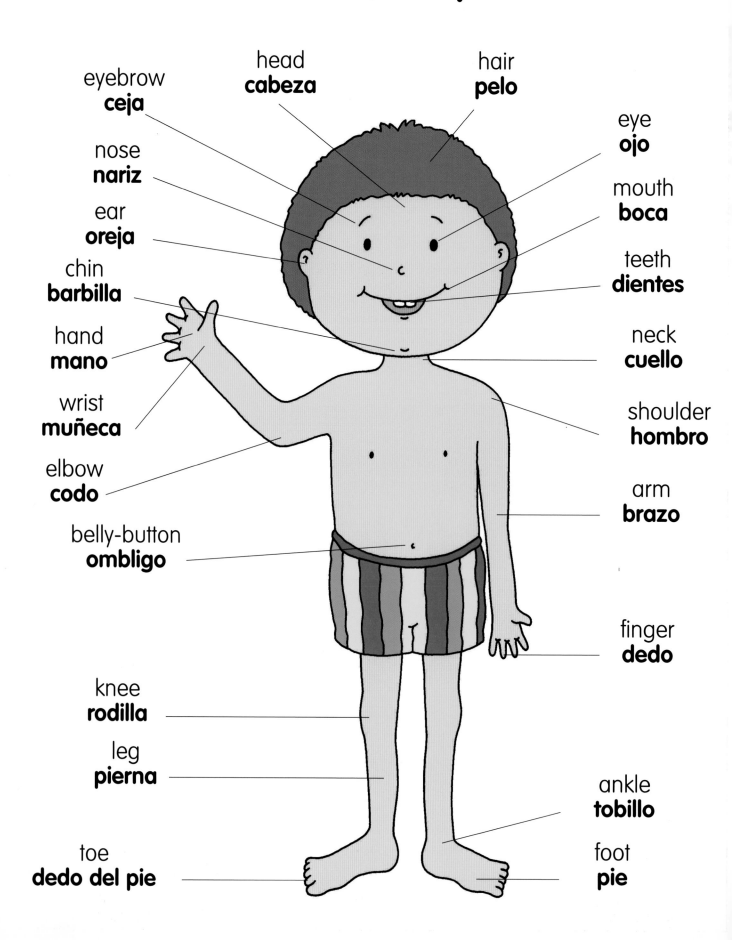

eyebrow **ceja**

head **cabeza**

hair **pelo**

nose **nariz**

eye **ojo**

ear **oreja**

mouth **boca**

chin **barbilla**

teeth **dientes**

hand **mano**

neck **cuello**

wrist **muñeca**

shoulder **hombro**

elbow **codo**

belly-button **ombligo**

arm **brazo**

knee **rodilla**

finger **dedo**

leg **pierna**

ankle **tobillo**

toe **dedo del pie**

foot **pie**

# What am I Doing? - ¿Qué hago?

I climb
**yo trepo**

I jump
**yo salto**

I blow
**yo soplo**

I swim
**yo nado**

I paint
**yo pinto**

I sit
**yo me siento**

I draw
**yo dibujo**

I skate
**yo patino**

I stand
**yo estoy de pie**

I slide
**yo me deslizo**

I dig
**yo cavo**

I write
**yo escribo**

I eat
**yo como**

I push
**yo empujo**

I swing
**yo me columpio**

I wash myself
**yo me lavo**

I drink
**yo bebo**

I sleep
**yo duermo**

# Wild Animals - Animales Salvajes

koala
**coala**

zebra
**cebra**

camel
**camello**

gorilla
**gorila**

kangaroo
**canguro**

hippopotamus
**hipopótamo**

crocodile
**cocodrilo**

monkey
**mono**

racoon
**mapache**

tiger
**tigre**

bear
**oso**

elephant
**elefante**

panda
**oso panda**

rhinoceros
**rinoceronte**

lion
**león**

snake
**serpiente**

iguana
**iguana**

polar
**oso polar**

giraffe
**jirafa**

beaver
**castor**

turtle
**tortuga marina**

# Pets and Birds - Animales domésticos y aves

hamster
**hámster**

tortoise
**tortuga**

chicken
**pollo**

ostrich
**avestruz**

peacock
**pavo real**

pony
**pony**

duck
**pato**

guinea pig
**conejillo de Indias**

dog
**perro**

rabbit
**conejo**

parrot
**loro**

fish
**pez**

penguin
**pingüino**

swan
**cisne**

mouse
**ratón**

canary
**canario**

cat
**gato**

pigeon
**paloma**

# Days, Months and Seasons - Días, Meses y Estaciones

Monday
**lunes**

Thursday
**jueves**

Saturday
**sábado**

Tuesday
**martes**

Friday
**viernes**

Sunday
**domingo**

Wednesday
**miércoles**

Spring
**primavera**

Summer
**verano**

Winter
**invierno**

Autumn
**otoño**

| January enero | February febrero | March marzo | April abril | May mayo | June junio |
|---|---|---|---|---|---|
| July julio | August agosto | September septiembre | October octubre | November noviembre | December diciembre |

# Opposites - Contrarios

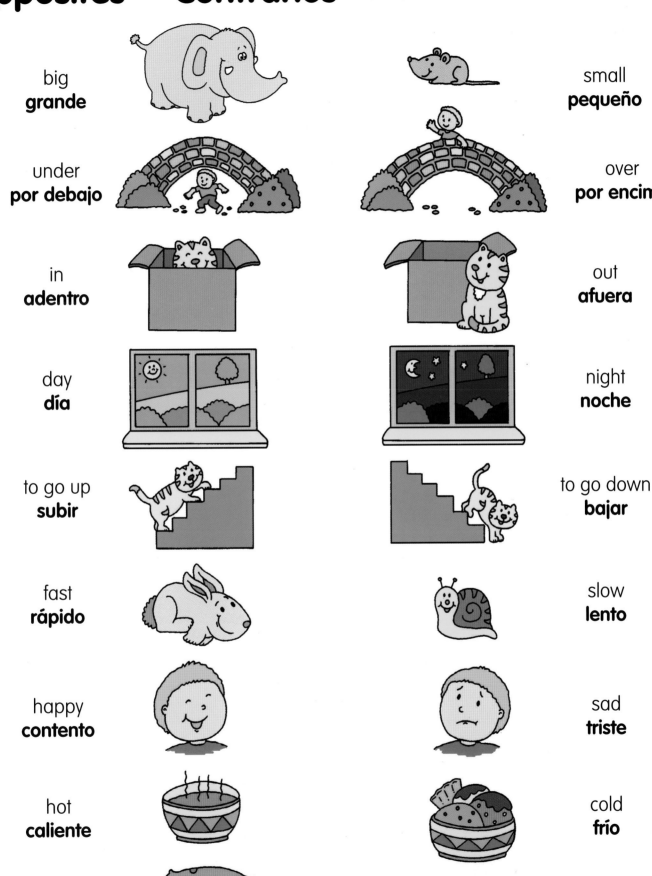

big
**grande**

small
**pequeño**

under
**por debajo**

over
**por encima**

in
**adentro**

out
**afuera**

day
**día**

night
**noche**

to go up
**subir**

to go down
**bajar**

fast
**rápido**

slow
**lento**

happy
**contento**

sad
**triste**

hot
**caliente**

cold
**frío**

soft
**blando**

hard
**duro**

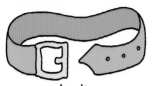

belt
**cinturón**

# Getting Dressed

shoes
**zapatos**

dress
**vestido**

blouse
**blusa**

socks
**medias**

hat
**sombrero**

skirt
**falda**

trousers
**pantalones**

coat
**abrigo**

sweater
**suéter**

t-shirt
**camiseta**

# Me Visto

scarf **bufanda**

ribbon **moño**

hanger **percha**

button **botón**

shelf **estante**

dungarees **overol**

jacket **chaqueta**

hook **gancho**

shorts **shorts**

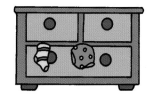
chest of drawers **cómoda**

zipper **zíper**

# Learn and Play

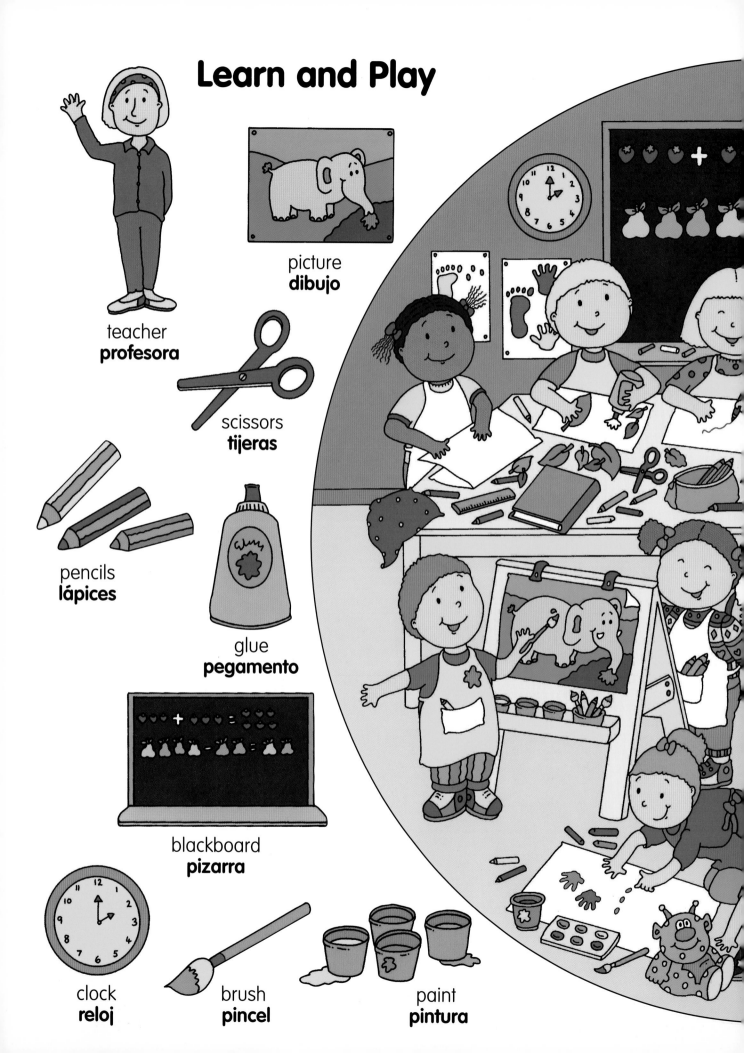

picture
**dibujo**

teacher
**profesora**

scissors
**tijeras**

pencils
**lápices**

glue
**pegamento**

blackboard
**pizarra**

clock
**reloj**

brush
**pincel**

paint
**pintura**

# Aprende y Juega

apron
**delantal**

dinosaur
**dinosaurio**

chalk
**tizas**

watercolors
**acuarelas**

table
**mesa**

crayons
**crayones**

cloth
**trapo**

plant
**planta**

paper
**papel**

book
**libro**

flag
**bandera**

woman
**mujer**

shells
**conchas**

boy
**niño**

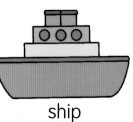

ship
**barco**

# At the Beach

towel
**toalla**

sandcastles
**castillos de arena**

seagull
**gaviota**

starfish
**estrella de mar**

ball
**pelota**

# En la Playa

lighthouse
**faro**

sand
**arena**

man
**hombre**

rocks
**rocas**

girl
**niña**

hat
**sombrero**

sunglasses
**lentes oscuros**

crab
**cangrejo**

bucket
**cubeta**

sea
**mar**

seaweed
**algas**

ice cream
**helado**

# Shopping

bread
**pan**

cucumbers
**pepinos**

eggs
**huevos**

cheese
**queso**

milk
**leche**

potatoes
**papas**

grapes
**uvas**

newspaper
**periódico**

oranges
**naranjas**

meat
**carne**

apples
**manzanas**

# Haciendo las Compras

sausages
**salchichas**

check-out
**caja**

basket
**canasta**

pears
**peras**

money
**dinero**

purse
**monedero**

bag
**bolsa**

flowers
**flores**

carrots
**zanahorias**

tomatoes
**tomates**

chocolate
**chocolate**

bananas
**plátanos**

# In the Garden

sprinkler
**aspersor**

rose
**rosa**

watering can
**regadera**

ant
**hormiga**

tree
**árbol**

cabbage
**repollo**

flower pot
**maceta**

lawnmower
**cortadora de césped**

lawn
**césped**

cat
**gato**

# En el jardín

sunflower
**girasol**

pond
**estanque**

nest
**nido**

leaves
**hojas**

bone
**hueso**

rake
**rastrillo**

dog
**perro**

bird
**pájaro**

bush
**arbusto**

wheelbarrow
**carretilla**

# At the Toy Store

jack-in-the-box
**caja de sorpresas**

doll
**muñeca**

teddy bear
**oso de peluche**

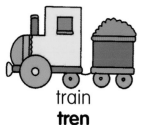

train
**tren**

jigsaw puzzle
**rompecabezas**

plane
**avión**

car
**coche**

drum
**tambor**

computer
**computadora**

blocks
**bloques**

# En la Juguetería

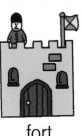

fort
**fuerte**

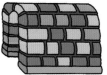

tunnel
**túnel**

truck
**camión**

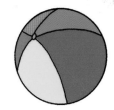

ball
**pelota**

yo yo
**yo-yo**

track
**vía de tren**

clown
**payaso**

trumpet
**trompeta**

helicopter
**helicóptero**

rocking horse
**caballo de balancín**

# A Rainy Day

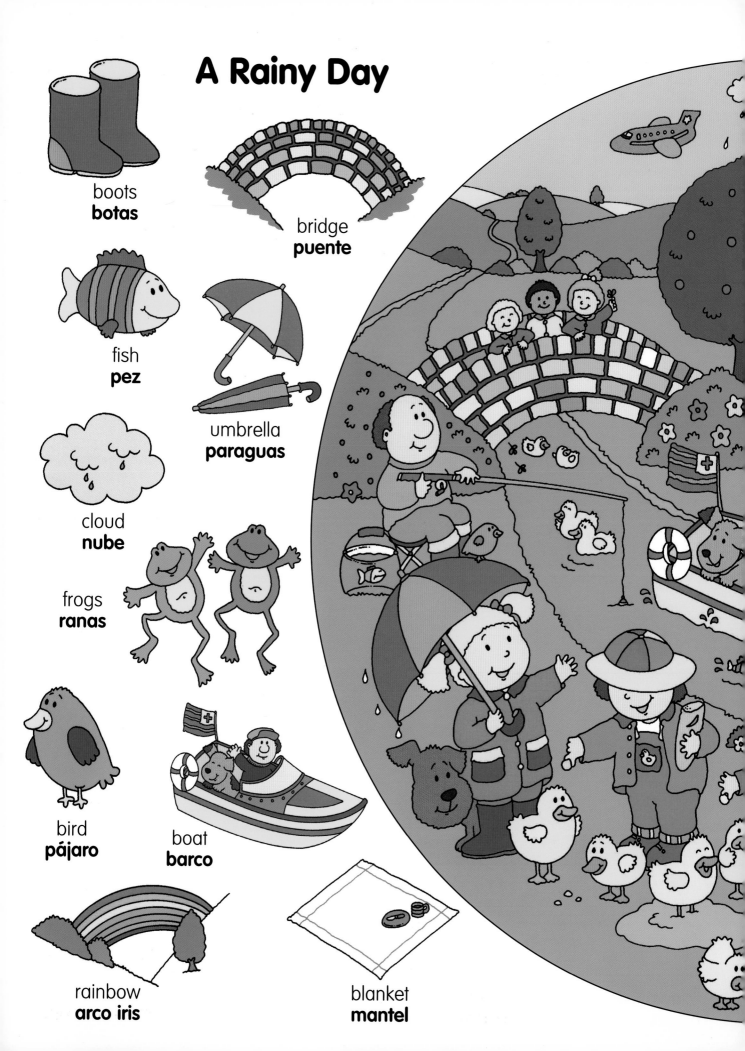

boots
**botas**

bridge
**puente**

fish
**pez**

umbrella
**paraguas**

cloud
**nube**

frogs
**ranas**

bird
**pájaro**

boat
**barco**

rainbow
**arco iris**

blanket
**mantel**

# Un día de lluvia

fence
**cerco**

wall
**pared**

train
**tren**

plane
**avión**

saucepan
**olla**

puddle
**charco**

rain hat
**gorro**

rain coat
**impermeable**

tent
**carpa**

scarecrow
**espantapájaros**

pig
**cerdo**

tractor
**tractor**

goat
**cabra**

# On the Farm

cobweb
**telaraña**

chicks
**pollitos**

duck
**pato**

horse
**caballo**

lamb
**cordero**

feathers
**plumas**

# En la granja

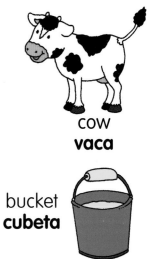
cow
**vaca**

bucket
**cubeta**
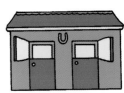

stable
**caballeriza**

turkey
**pavo**

goose
**oca**

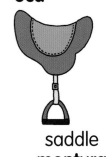
saddle
**montura**

pig sty
**pocilga**

barn
**granero**

farmer
**granjero**

dog
**perro**

pond
**estanque**

# Playing in the snow

ice skates
**patines**

skis
**esquís**

hat
**gorro**

snowman
**muñeco de nieve**

mittens
**mitones**

bird
**pájaro**

icicle
**carámbano**

jacket
**chaqueta**

snowballs
**bolas de nieve**

iceberg
**iceberg**

# Jugando en la Nieve

gloves
**guantes**

coat
**abrigo**

scarf
**bufanda**

igloo
**iglú**

mountains
**montañas**

snowflakes
**copos de nieve**

Eskimo
**esquimal**

toboggan
**trineo**

trees
**árboles**

# On the Riverbank

fish
**pez**

rabbit
**conejo**

bees
**abejas**

tadpole
**renacuajos**

jar
**tarro**

frogs
**ranas**

fishing pole
**caña de pescar**

net
**red**

butterflies
**mariposas**

# A la Orilla del Río

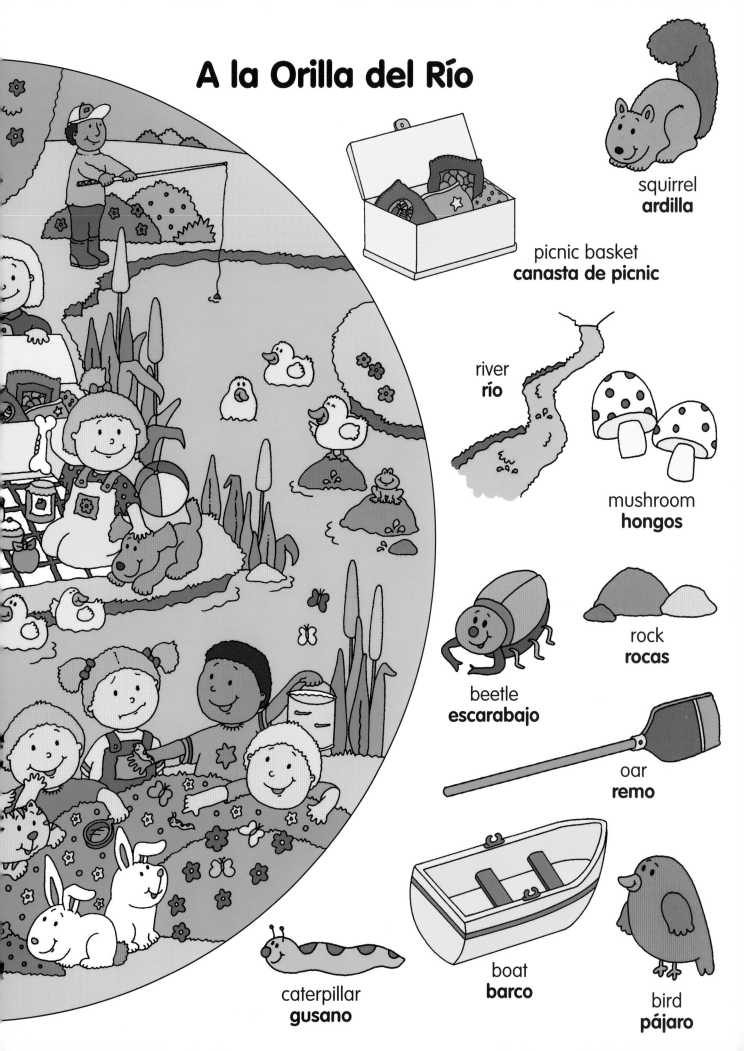

squirrel
**ardilla**

picnic basket
**canasta de picnic**

river
**río**

mushroom
**hongos**

beetle
**escarabajo**

rock
**rocas**

oar
**remo**

caterpillar
**gusano**

boat
**barco**

bird
**pájaro**

kite
**papalote**

fountain
**fuente**

boat
**barco**

# In the Park

swing
**columpio**

see-saw
**resbaladilla**

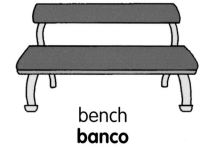

bench
**banco**

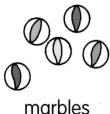

marbles
**canicas**

# En el Parque

buggy
**carreola**

scooter
**patin del Diablo**

slide
**tobogán**

bicycle
**bicicleta**

skates
**patines**

ball
**pelota**

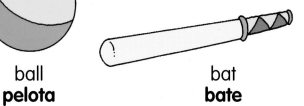

bat
**bate**

sandbox
**cajón de arena**

# In the Kitchen

stove
**cocina**

flour
**harina**

butter
**mantequilla**

mixing bowl
**recipiente**

chopping board
**tabla de picar**

dishwasher
**lavavajillas**

rolling pin
**rodillo**

cup
**taza**

apron
**delantal**

wooden spoon
**cuchara de madera**

# En la Cocina

microwave
**microondas**

chair
**silla**

sink
**fregadero**

glass
**vaso**

fork
**tenedor**

spoon
**cuchara**

knife
**cuchillo**

toaster
**tostadora**

table
**mesa**

plate
**plato**

cake **pastel**

sandwiches **emparedados**

balloon **globo**

cookies **galletas**

# The Birthday Party

presents **regalos**

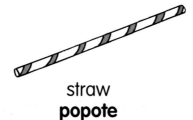

straw **popote**

ice cream **helado**

party hats **gorros de fiesta**

# La Fiesta de Cumpleaños

milk
**leche**

necklace
**collar**

cards
**tarjetas**

candle
**vela**

popcorn
**esquites**

tablecloth
**mantel**

camera
**máquina fotográfica**

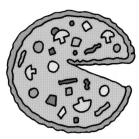

pizza
**pizza**

# Time for Bed

stars
**estrellas**

mirror
**espejo**

brush
**cepillo**

comb
**peine**

bath
**bañera**

sponge
**esponja**

soap
**jabón**

owl
**búho**

towel
**toalla**

toothbrush
**cepillo de dientes**

toothpaste
**pasta de dientes**

# Hora de ir a Dormir

picture
**retrato**

toys
**juguetes**

pillow
**almohada**

bed
**cama**

sheet
**sábana**

lamp
**lámpara**

storybook
**libro de cuentos**

teddy bear
**oso de peluche**

shoes
**pantuflas**

rug
**alfombra**

# Dictionary = Diccionario

## Counting to twenty
one = **uno**
two = **dos**
three = **tres**
four = **cuatro**
five = **cinco**
six = **seis**

seven = **siete**
eight = **ocho**
nine = **nueve**
ten = **diez**
eleven = **once**
twelve = **doce**
thirteen = **trece**

fourteen = **catorce**
fifteen = **quince**
sixteen = **dieciséis**
seventeen = **dieciseite**
eighteen = **dieciocho**
nineteen = **diecinueve**
twenty = **veinte**

## Shapes and Colors
blue = **azul**
orange = **naranja**
yellow = **amarillo**
red = **rojo**
green = **verde**
brown = **marrón**

black = **negro**
white = **blanco**
pink = **rosa**
purple = **morado**
circle = **círculo**
rectangle = **rectángulo**
diamond = **rombo**

triangle = **triángulo**
square = **cuadrado**
oval = **óvalo**
semi-circle = **semicírculo**
crescent = **media luna**
heart = **corazón**
star = **estrella**

## Our Bodies
chin = **barbilla**
mouth = **boca**
arm = **brazo**
head = **cabeza**
eyebrow = **ceja**
elbow = **codo**
neck = **cuello**

finger = **dedo**
toe = **dedo del pie**
teeth = **dientes**
shoulder = **hombro**
hand = **mano**
wrist = **muñeca**
nose = **nariz**
eye = **ojo**

belly-button = **ombligo**
ear = **oreja**
hair = **pelo**
foot = **pie**
leg = **pierna**
knee = **rodilla**
ankle = **tobillo**

## What am I Doing?
I climb = **yo trepo**
I jump = **yo salto**
I blow = **yo soplo**
I swim = **yo nado**
I paint = **yo pinto**
I sit = **yo me siento**

I draw = **yo dibujo**
I skate = **yo patino**
I stand = **yo estoy de pie**
I slide = **yo me deslizo**
I dig = **yo cavo**
I write = **yo escribo**
I eat = **yo como**

I push = **yo empujo**
I swing = **yo me columpio**
I wash myself = **yo me lavo**
I drink = **yo bebo**
I sleep = **yo duermo**

## Wild Animals
camel = **camello**
beaver = **castor**
zebra = **cebra**

koala = **coala**
crocodile = **cocodrilo**
elephant = **elefante**
gorilla = **gorila**
hippopotamus = **hipopótamo**
iguana = **iguana**
giraffe = **jirafa**
kangaroo = **canguro**
lion = **león**

racoon = **mapache**
monkey = **mono**
bear = **oso**
polar = **oso polar**
panda = **oso panda**
rhinoceros = **rinoceronte**
snake = **serpiente**
tiger = **tigre**
turtle = **tortuga marina**

## Pets and Birds

ostrich = **avestruz**
canary = **canario**
swan = **cisne**
guinea pig = **conejillo de Indias**
rabbit = **conejo**
cat = **gato**
hamster = **hámster**

pony = **pony**
parrot = **loro**
pigeon = **paloma**
duck = **pato**
peacock = **pavo real**
penguin = **pingüino**
dog = **perro**
fish = **pez**

chicken = **pollo**
mouse = **ratón**
tortoise = **tortuga**

## Days, Months and Seasons

Monday = **lunes**
Tuesday = **martes**
Wednesday = **miércoles**
Thursday = **jueves**
Friday = **viernes**
Saturday = **sábado**
Sunday = **domingo**

Spring = **primavera**
Summer = **verano**
Autumn = **otoño**
Winter = **invierno**
January = **enero**
February = **febrero**
March = **marzo**
April = **abril**

May = **mayo**
June = **junio**
July = **julio**
August = **agosto**
September = **septiembre**
October = **octubre**
November = **noviembre**
December = **diciembre**

## Opposites

big = **grande**
under = **por debajo**
in = **adentro**
day = **día**
to go up = **subir**
fast = **rápido**
happy = **contento**
hot = **caliente**
soft = **blando**

small = **pequeño**
over = **por encima**
out = **afuera**
night = **noche**
to go down = **bajar**
slow = **lento**
sad = **triste**
cold = **frio**
hard = **duro**

## Getting Dressed

coat = **abrigo**
blouse = **blusa**
button = **botón**
scarf = **bufanda**
socks = **medias**
t-shirt = **camiseta**
jacket = **chaqueta**

belt = **cinturón**
hook = **gancho**
chest of drawers = **cómoda**
zipper = **zíper**
shelf = **estante**
skirt = **falda**
sweater = **suéter**
ribbon = **mōno**

dungarees = **overol**
trousers = **pantalones**
shorts = **shorts**
hanger = **percha**
hat = **sombrero**
dress = **vestido**
shoes = **zapatos**

### Learn and Play
watercolors = **acuarelas**
crayons = **crayones**
apron = **delantal**
picture = **dibujo**
dinosaur = **dinosaurio**
pencils = **lápices**

book = **libro**
table = **mesa**
paper = **papel**
glue = **pegamento**
brush = **pincel**
paint = **pintura**
blackboard = **pizarra**

plant = **planta**
teacher = **profesora**
clock = **reloj**
scissors = **tijeras**
chalk = **tizas**
cloth = **trapo**

### At the Beach
seaweed = **algas**
sand = **arena**
flag = **bandera**
ship = **barco**
crab = **cangrejo**
sandcastles = **castillos de arena**
shells = **conchas**

bucket = **cubeta**
starfish = **estrella de mar**
lighthouse = **faro**
seagull = **gaviota**
sunglasses = **lentes oscuros**
ice cream = **helado**
man = **hombre**
sea = **mar**

woman = **mujer**
girl = **niña**
boy = **niño**
ball = **pelota**
rocks = **rocas**
hat = **sombrero**
towel = **toalla**

### Shopping
bag = **bolsa**
check-out = **caja**
meat = **carne**
basket = **canasta**
chocolate = **chocolate**
money = **dinero**
flowers = **flores**

eggs = **huevos**
milk = **leche**
apples = **manzanas**
purse = **monedero**
oranges = **naranjas**
bread = **pan**
potatoes = **papas**
cucumbers = **pepinos**

pears = **peras**
newspaper = **periódico**
bananas = **plátanos**
cheese = **queso**
sausages = **salchichas**
tomatoes = **tomates**
grapes = **uvas**
carrots = **zanahorias**

### In the Garden
tree = **árbol**
bush = **arbusto**
wheelbarrow = **carretilla**
lawn = **césped**
cabbage = **repollo**
lawnmower = **cortadora de cespéd**
pond = **estanque**
cat = **gato**
sunflower = **girasol**

leaves = **hojas**
ant = **hormiga**
bone = **hueso**
flower pot = **maceta**
nest = **nido**
bird = **pájaro**
dog = **perro**
rake = **rastrillo**
watering can = **regadera**
sprinkler = **aspersor**
rose = **rosa**

## At the Toy Store
plane = **avión**
blocks = **bloques**
rocking horse =
**caballo de balancín**
jack-in-the-box =
**caja de sorpresas**
truck = **camión**

car = **coche**
fort = **fuerte**
helicopter = **helicóptero**
doll = **muñeca**
computer = **computadora**
teddy bear = **oso de peluche**
clown = **payaso**
ball = **pelota**

jigsaw puzzle = **rompecabezas**
drum = **tambor**
train = **tren**
trumpet = **trompeta**
tunnel = **túnel**
track = **vía de tren**
yo yo = **yo-yo**

## A Rainy Day
rainbow = **arco iris**
plane = **avión**
boat = **barco**
boots = **botas**
puddle = **charco**
rain hat = **gorro**

rain coat = **impermeable**
blanket = **mantel**
cloud = **nube**
saucepan = **olla**
bird = **pájaro**
umbrella = **paraguas**
wall = **pared**

fish = **pez**
bridge = **puente**
frogs = **ranas**
tent = **carpa**
train = **tren**
fence = **cerco**

## On the Farm
horse = **caballo**
goat = **cabra**
pig = **cerdo**
lamb = **cordero**
stable = **caballeriza**
bucket = **cubeta**
scarecrow = **espantapájaros**

pond = **estanque**
barn = **granero**
farmer = **granjero**
goose = **oca**
duck = **pato**
turkey = **pavo**
dog = **perro**
feathers = **plumas**

pig sty = **pocilga**
chicks = **pollitos**
saddle = **montura**
cobweb = **telaraña**
tractor = **tractor**
cow = **vaca**

## Playing in the Snow
coat = **abrigo**
trees = **árboles**
snowballs = **bolas de nieve**
scarf = **bufanda**
icicle = **carámbano**
jacket = **chaqueta**
snowflakes = **copos de nieve**
skis = **esquís**
Eskimo = **esquimal**

hat = **gorro**
gloves = **guantes**
iceberg = **iceberg**
igloo = **iglú**
mountains = **montañas**
snowman = **muñeco de nieve**
bird = **pájaro**
ice skates = **patines**
mittens = **mitones**
toboggan = **trineo**

## On the Riverbank

bees = **abejas**
squirrel = **ardilla**
boat = **barco**
fishing pole = **caña de pescar**
picnic basket = **canasta de picnic**

rabbit = **conejo**
beetle = **escarabajo**
caterpillar = **gusano**
butterfly = **mariposa**
bird = **pájaro**
fish = **pez**
frogs = **ranas**

net = **red**
oar = **remo**
tadpole = **renacuajos**
river = **río**
rock = **roca**
mushroom = **hongos**
jar = **tarro**

## In the Park

see-saw = **resbaladilla**
bench = **banco**
boat = **barco**
bicycle = **bicicleta**
sandbox = **cajón de arena**
marbles = **canicas**
swing = **columpio**

kite = **papalote**
fountain = **fuente**
bat = **bate**
skates = **patines**
scooter = **patín del Diablo**
ball = **pelota**
buggy = **carreola**
slide = **tobogán**

## In the Kitchen

stove = **cocina**
spoon = **cuchara**
wooden spoon = **cuchara de madera**
knife = **cuchillo**
mixing bowl = **recipiente**
apron = **delantal**

sink = **fregadero**
flour = **harina**
dishwasher = **lavavajillas**
butter = **mantequilla**
table = **mesa**
microwave = **microondas**
plate = **plato**
chair = **silla**

chopping board = **tabla de picar**
toaster = **tostadora**
cup = **taza**
fork = **tenedor**
rolling pin = **rodillo**
glass = **vaso**

## The Birthday Party

sandwiches = **emparedados**
necklace = **collar**
cookies = **galletas**
balloon = **globo**
party hat = **gorro de fiesta**
ice cream = **helado**

milk = **leche**
tablecloth = **mantel**
camera = **máquina fotográfica**
straw = **popote**
popcorn = **esquites**
cake = **pastel**
pizza = **pizza**

presents = **regalos**
cards = **tarjetas**
candle = **vela**

## Time for Bed

rug = **alfombra**
pillow = **almohada**
bath = **bañera**
owl = **búho**
bed = **cama**
brush = **cepillo**
toothbrush = **cepillo de dientes**

mirror = **espejo**
sponge = **esponja**
stars = **estrellas**
soap = **jabón**
toys = **juguetes**
lamp = **lámpara**
storybook = **libro de cuentos**
teddy bear = **oso de peluche**

toothpaste = **pasta de dientes**
comb = **peine**
picture = **retrato**
sheet = **sábana**
towel = **toalla**
shoes = **pantuflas**

# How to say Spanish words in this book (pronunciation)

Spanish letters are often pronounced differently to English letters, although some are very similar. The following letters should be pronounced as though they are English letters:

**b, d, f, k, l, m, n, p, s, t,** plus the grouping **ch**

The follow letters are a little more difficult, but with practice it will start to come naturally:

## Vowels

**a** as in the 'a' in cat
**e** as in the 'e' in den
**i** as in the 'ea' in team
**o** as in the 'o' in pot
**u** as in the 'oo' in boot

## Consonants

**c + e** or **i** as 's'
**c** (followed by any other letter) as in the 'c' in cage
**g + e** or **i** as in the 'ch' in loch
**gue** or **gui** as in the 'g' in 'go'
**g** (followed by any other letter) as in the 'g' in 'go'
**h** is always silent, so just skip the letter when saying it
**j** as in the 'ch' in loch
**ll** sounds like 'l' and 'y' together, as in the 'll' in million
**ñ** as in the 'n' in onion
**q** (always followed by u) as in the 'k' in king
**r** is rolled, like rr (properly rolled r's will have your tongue flapping!)
**rr** is rolled more – like rrrr
**v** as in the 'b' in baby
**w** as in the 'v' in van
**z** as in the 'th' in thin